empower

publishing

Also from Empower Publishing

by Linwood Best

Best "Quotes"

Best "Sayings"

Thoughts on Paper

publish.empower.now@gmail.com

Learn to Listen, Listen to Learn

By

Linwood Best

Empower Publishing

Winston-Salem

Empower Publishing
302 Ricks Drive
Winston-Salem, NC 27103

First Empower Publishing Books edition published September, 2024
Empower Publishing, Feather Pen, and all production design are trademarks of Indigo Sea Press, used under license.

For information regarding bulk purchases of this book, digital purchase and special discounts, please contact the publisher at publish.empower.now@gmail.com

Cover design by Linwood Best
Manufactured in the United States of America
ISBN 978-1-63066-610-1

TABLE OF CONTENTS

On many occasions and during sessions, I asked the question. What is worse, someone not listening or someone refusing to talk? You can imagine the different responses supported by their own theory, notion, and expectation.

It seems to happen when you thought you had made headway. Somehow, instead, you discovered that you were not on the highway. Was it because someone ran through the red light, did not yield, or made the wrong turn? This can happen when we assume rather than listen. It reminds me of the question my daughter asked, "Dad, do people listen for information or to respond?" Rather than asking for clarity and welcomed dialogue or a window of opportunity, instead there is a revolving door to ineffective communication. Surprisingly, an unfamiliar language has taken on a different voice and tone. Words have lost their meaning, and confusion has followed with an expression of itself. Words, if not understood or grasped, are like the fastest runner running a race but running in the wrong direction. He or she might have the fastest time, but to no avail. The record stands for itself; they may be the record holder, but not this time. "In all thy getting, get an understanding." You will never be able to effectively share an ideal, love, thought, or feeling if both parties don't get it. Get it? Communication does not record speed but completion. Run the race, but pace yourself.

According to the Help Guide, "Effective communication is about more than just exchanging information. It's about understanding the emotion and intentions behind the information. As well as being able to clearly convey a message, you need to also listen in a way that gains the full meaning of what's being said and makes the other person feel heard and understood."

My first aid kit for this is my personal and favorite quote: learn to listen and listen to learn. I have listened and learned how they have been interpreted and misinterpreted. How in the world could this happen? "I know what I said. "True, you may, but were you understood?

How often do we ask for clarity? Assumption is a road traveled without noticing the signs. Like a road sign, we need to be just as attentive to our words as the people in the audience. Words are powerful; however listening will hit the target. Remember, many people find it very difficult to express themselves. For some, the best you will get is a short sentence. A quote for them is like an introduction or standing terrified before a crowd.

Again, I feel privileged to have you step outside of the box and discover how people may think alike but express themselves differently. We might not prefer to use a map or GPS, but the focus is to reach the destination. Optimistically, we will gain an appreciation and acceptance for diversity. Words take on a different meaning, especially when we are ignorant of their origin. After all, "I can dig it" does not require a shovel.

Several people have used these phrases when they were lost for words as icebreakers. Others say they were used to stimulate thought during times of reflection and mediation in group sessions.

Some have said they used them as the third person. From me to you, my hope is that you find something that fits you. Space has been provided for you to jot down your thoughts for whatever you like. Enjoy.

Encouragement

Excuses need a place to hide and be quiet. They are presented unexpectedly but take off when questioned.

_____

_____

_____

_____

_____

Excuses hasten to speak first.

_____

_____

_____

_____

Get a room and a window before you imprison your mind. There might not be another chance.

_____

_____

_____

_____

_____

God will always give you more than you ask for if you are willing to wait.

_____

_____

_____

_____

Longevity is longer than now. So, look beyond yesterday.

Without compromise, there will never be a resolution.

An excuse is not a pardon but rather an opportunity to delay getting things right.

To recover from a fall starts with a helping hand.

If life waits for no one, we should not waste time. Cherish it because we cannot get it back.

For there to be longevity in your relationship, treat it like ordering eggs on the menu. Rather than scramble hard, request that they be over easy or sunny side up.

It is better to say see you later than goodbye. Next time could open the door for possibilities.

If honesty brings truth to light, then darkness should never become a champion.

Compassion when needed and not received is like filling a prescription and not taking the medicine.

Excuses are dead set against correction and wrestle with the thought of being guilty.

When we don't have much time, we realize the importance of how to use it; when there seems to be ample time, we abuse it. Time is a measure not to be misconstrued.

_____

_____

_____

_____

_____

_____

In order for something to be noteworthy, take notes.

_____

_____

_____

_____

_____

A welcome conversation is like background music; it has your complete attention.

_____

_____

_____

_____

_____

Excuses rarely if ever welcome questions or discussions. When discovered, excuses hasten to speak first.

_____

_____

_____

_____

_____

Getting what you want is an endorsement beyond your needs.

I would rather have a smoothie than an argument.

Don't let others help you to make a mistake. You will have to live with it after they have jumped ship.

Abandonment and neglect will never admit that they are kith and kin, but the evidence will prove otherwise.

Wishful thinking is a teaser to the imagination, but reality is its quest.

_____

_____

_____

_____

_____

_____

Artificial resuscitation is a temporary procedure to revive me; only love will sustain me.

_____

_____

_____

_____

_____

_____

Excuses should be short-lived, honest, and never a badge of courage. Its goal is to display humility.

_____

_____

_____

_____

_____

_____

Don't leave me in suspense; tell me the truth; otherwise, keep it to yourself.

_____

_____

_____

_____

_____

_____

Truth for deaf ears is worse than lies skirting themselves just to be heard.

_____

_____

_____

_____

_____

_____

There will be trials and then triumph; beware, behind triumph there will be trials.

_____

_____

_____

_____

_____

_____

A fib should never be used as a cover-up. Nor should it silence others.

_____

_____

_____

_____

_____

_____

I may not have the fastest horse, but I have never lost a race.

_____

_____

_____

_____

_____

Confusion is like putting eye drops in your mouth so that you can see what others are saying.

_____

_____

_____

_____

_____

Technology has made it almost impossible to have a free hand.

_____

_____

_____

_____

_____

Mental illness's ultimate therapy is having someone listen without a quick fix or general anesthesia.

_____

_____

_____

_____

_____

_____

It is risky but worth it to begin again because we seldom get the chance.

_____

_____

_____

_____

_____

Excuses are always appropriate for the user but should provide clarity to the receiving or listening party.

_____

_____

_____

_____

_____

Hope and love have never been more needful than today. Perhaps it is the only solution for this troubled world.

_____

_____

_____

_____

_____

A smile and a laugh will change the facial expression, but the heart will confirm the distinction by the reaction.

_____

_____

_____

_____

_____

_____

It is hard to get to know someone who does not remember your name.

_____

_____

_____

_____

_____

_____

An assumption is often valid without a response.

As long as we have covered memories, they will only be fantasy.

The difference between insurance and assurance is that you pay for one to get the other.

In silence we learn to be attentive in hopes to see if others are listening.

Knowing is better than believing.

_____
_____
_____
_____
_____
_____

Ask a child where someone lives in the neighborhood, and
soon you will discover how little you know your neighbors.

_____
_____
_____
_____
_____
_____

Life might not be a boxing match, but you have to gear up.

Marriage can only be manageable when the two of you decide to tackle life together.

For you to be successful you must attend the course of action to be promoted.

Modus operandi is not a one for all.

When-speaking remember, that some people might be wearing hearing aids.

Music is a healthy distraction and should not need a personal invitation.

Reality won't let your secrets stay hidden.

People cannot change when you don't give them a chance.

A good way to overcome struggles is to dream.

Never let yesterday outline your tomorrow's.

Underneath doubt are hidden possibilities.

A promise should be a guarantee rather than an unfulfilled wish.

Enticement

Forgiveness is difficult to see in the rear view.

_____
_____
_____
_____
_____
_____

When we opt out to be open, we cancel the discovery of our similarities.

_____
_____
_____
_____

The saddest word after saying, "I do" is "I did."

Imagine how your parents would rejoice to see the reflection of their labor of love manifest.

Nonchalant is like listening to hours of music and not remembering one song.

Deception from a friend is like walking in the woods; we have to watch out for the snakes in the grass.

_____

_____

I can accept it if you overcharged me by mistake, but cheating me intentionally should be a crime.

_____

_____

_____

_____

_____

The route back after a heartbreak will require healing and restored self-assurance. Otherwise, grief will take residence.

_____

_____

_____

_____

_____

Godly living is better than a personal trainer.

_____

_____

_____

_____

_____

Forgiven individuals should never forget how to forgive.

_____

_____

_____

_____

_____

21

The thought of remembering is wonderful when so many try to forget.

_____

_____

_____

_____

_____

_____

Aims are notions that are sidelined if not acted on.

_____

_____

_____

_____

_____

Confidence is a natural byproduct of clarity. What + why + who = how and when.

_____

_____

It is a good idea to start, but to finish is greater.

There is no need for justification for doing what is right.

When we stop trusting God, we have come to the end of the road.

Being double-minded is like being pulled in different directions at the same time with stretch marks to show.

Thinking about it too long just might end up lost. Decide and adjust if needed.

It is better to compromise and grow rather than always being right and remaining alone.

Remember to let the valley be our temporary quarters. There is higher ground for those who keep climbing.

Extrovert, introvert, ambivert, or a combination of all three is who you might be, and that is okay. Self-discovery is what matters most.

_____

_____

_____

_____

_____

_____

It is not the struggles of life that are difficult; it is not being able to share them.

_____

_____

_____

_____

_____

You don't have to know everything; time will determine if there is a need.

Hurt will cause you to become helpful or hateful.

Dialogue with some people is like a pop quiz. We often fail trying to answer the question without giving it our undivided attention.

Create an environment that allows freedom. You just might get the right answer.

You cannot sleep nor ignore compassion. You either have it or you don't.

_____

_____

_____

_____

_____

_____

_____

Because you are talking and have authority does not mean you are being heard.

_____

_____

_____

_____

_____

_____

Reinforcement and backup are needed when there is no confrontation. It is like going over the same thing unnecessarily.

_____

_____

_____

_____

_____

_____

Cooperation will go a lot further than competition. Rivalry is a match for disaster.

_____

_____

_____

_____

_____

_____

_____

You may forget someone's actions but not their words. It is better to get it right than be right.

_____

_____

_____

_____

_____

_____

_____

The request of life is being taken, place your order now.

_____

_____

_____
_____
_____
_____
_____

Worrying does not add anything to your life, but it can subtract from it. It is intentional without benefit.

_____
_____
_____
_____
_____

Falling in love after being hurt is like climbing Mount Everest without a rope. They both are a challenge to the heart and have slippery slopes.

_____
_____
_____
_____
_____

As long as someone else knows what you know, there can never be a secret.

_____
_____
_____
_____
_____

29

Backsliding is searching for what you left behind.

Rejection does not have final authority unless you accept it as denial.

Hidden between love and lust is loneliness.

Identity theft should not be confused with imitation of another person. Even with identical twins, they are different. Be the self that you can be, it is easier.

_____

_____

_____

_____

_____

Always interview people before you consider them to become a part of your inner circle.

_____

_____

_____

_____

_____

_____

There should never be expectation when there is no sign of a future.

_____

_____

_____

_____

_____

_____

We would probably save a lot of time and hardship if we would ask, Why?

_____

_____

_____

_____

_____

_____

If the words I love you cause you to stutter, trip over your tongue, or not respond, thank you in advance.

_____

_____

_____

_____

_____

_____

_____

We should not want God's promises without practicing his will.

_____

_____

_____

_____

_____

_____

_____

We will be unable to distinguish God's voice if we have little dialog with him.

_____

_____

_____

_____

_____

Begging God could be an indication that we need a righteous investigation.

_____

_____

_____

_____

_____

_____

_____

Humility is great, but foolishness is not to be tolerated.

_____

_____

_____

_____

_____

_____

_____

People normally look at the size of the vehicle rather than the skill of the driver.

_____

_____

_____

_____

_____

_____

_____

As puzzling as you make it, in time I will figure it out.

_____

_____

_____

_____

_____

_____

_____

I heard you the first time, but I love you so much that I want to hear it again.

_____

_____

_____

_____

_____

_____

_____

Anybody can be had, but I have been taken.

_____

_____

_____

_____

If God does not have respect of person, then I will get back in line.

Nothing next to nothing is nothing, but something without nothing is still something without nothing.

Pride tried to make friends with joy, pride left.

There cannot be a new beginning without a fresh start.

Boldness is having the courage to do what I desire to be done for me.

We stop hiding when we accept our past as the past. It happened; now let's move on.

When two people cannot decide what to do, take a vote that we need to do something.

Expressive

Just when I thought I could not take it anymore, God showed I could, and I did.

_____

_____

_____

_____

_____

_____

_____

Leave me alone while I still have respect for you.

_____

_____

_____

_____

_____

_____

Life can be compared to basketball, pass, or shoot.

_____

_____

_____

_____

_____

_____

I will call when I need you: if I don't call I don't need you.

_____

_____

Time may have passed, but the message is the same. Don't waste it.

I rather be sure of what I heard than wonder what you are thinking.

I am not mean, just frank.

Friendship is by permission only.

_____

_____

_____

_____

_____

_____

Crying is tough, but we must know when to stop.

_____

_____

_____

_____

_____

_____

You might have survived, but the learned lesson is proof you got it.

_____

_____

_____

_____

_____

_____

The rest of your life is up to you.

_____

_____

_____

_____

_____

Resolve the issue before the tears dry.

_____

_____

_____

_____

_____

I am not worried anymore because I have cried, been truthful, and still you refuse to listen.

_____

_____

_____

_____

_____

Two things can break up a marriage: stuff and other people.

___

There is a boomerang in life; don't let it hit you. Watch out; here it comes again.

___

The trails of life sometimes can be grueling, but still there's more get-up-and-go.

___

How critical you are will depend on what really matters.

___

You keep telling me your dislikes. For some reason, I did not get the hint.

_____
_____
_____
_____
_____
_____
_____
_____

Joy is contingent on doing the will of God. He only knows what is yet to come.

_____
_____
_____
_____
_____
_____
_____
_____

Unfaithfulness in marriage can be a flagrant foul or a cause for ejection.

Belief requires a total commitment, or doubt will present a false reward.

Challenges are opportunities to be certain of consequences.

_____

_____

_____

_____

_____

_____

_____

Commitment is a willingness to stay the course at all costs.

_____

_____

_____

_____

_____

_____

Confidence is like faith in that it expects a favorable outcome.

_____

_____

_____

_____

_____

_____

Courage expects victory without an excuse.

_____

_____

_____

_____

_____

_____

45

Dare does not need assistance; it will go alone.

_____
_____
_____
_____
_____
_____
_____

People remember what is said with or without documentation. It pays to be truthful; otherwise, there is zero credit.

_____
_____
_____
_____
_____
_____
_____

It is okay to glance in life's rearview mirror, but stay focused on what's ahead.

_____
_____
_____
_____
_____
_____
_____

You may give someone an answer, but they must find the truth.

_____
_____
_____
_____

_____

_____

_____

Don't return to the scene of the crime; you might be
identified.

_____

_____

_____

_____

_____

_____

We can always learn from the past when we admit it.

_____

_____

_____

_____

_____

_____

The storms of life are like the sea; peace is the solution.

_____

_____

_____

_____

_____

_____

Always be looking, but don't be desperate.

_____

_____

_____

_____

_____

_____

I understand the strength I have when I pray for others, especially my enemies.

_____

_____

_____

_____

_____

_____

The more attentive we are, the clearer God's voice is. We'll distinguish his voice from others even in a crowd.

_____

_____

_____

_____

_____
_____
_____

The advantage of time alone with God gives us a greater appreciation for His presence.

_____
_____
_____
_____
_____
_____

Your life importance will be reflected by your legacy. It will be cherished by those who are benefited by the mantle that has been passed.

_____
_____
_____
_____
_____
_____

If you did not understand what I thought I understood, let's talk about it.

_____
_____
_____
_____
_____
_____

49

You can't appreciate what you have until you no longer have it.

_____
_____
_____
_____
_____
_____
_____
_____

When there is a need for good intention, a sense of duty is not a substitute.

_____
_____
_____
_____

Eyes of neglect and an unconcern attitude are as death to a dying soul.

If you are not familiar with disappointment, you will not know how to adjust.

Only when you suspect danger are you fearful.

An honest answer is better than a reasonable conclusion.

Logic has no place where faith is needed.

It is impossible to love someone else when you dislike yourself.

We hurt others with pain from our past.

You will never arrive if you don't start. Starting might be slow, but finishing is in view.

_____

_____

_____

_____

_____

_____

_____

Only when you are compassionate can you understand how someone feels.

_____

_____

_____

_____

_____

_____

_____

Without the counsel of God, it is like shopping. You may find your size, and still it does not fit.

_____

_____

_____

_____

_____

_____

_____

We will never find what we do not seek.

_____

_____

_____

Gossip is good seemingly for the moment; beware, there will be consequences.

God might alter the process but not the progress.

_____

_____

_____

With God, you can use a putter in a sand trap.

_____

_____

_____

_____

_____

_____

An excuse is an addiction that runs out of apology.

_____

_____

_____

_____

_____

_____

A physical attraction without a scriptural connection is equivalent to a hot fuzzy.

_____

_____

_____

_____

_____

_____

Staying focused when the view is blurred is an indication that we need to get God's insight.

_____

_____

People will accept man's promise before they will believe God's truth.

Our plans may change. It is better to check with God, his are guarantees.

The three foundations for accomplishment are: decision-willing-commit.

_____

_____

Love is like good credit and a debt that needs to be paid. You make the payment, but you never want to close the account.

_____

_____

_____

_____

_____

_____

_____

The classroom of life despite absenteeism, tardiness, and failures is not the true representation of one's potential.

_____

_____

_____

_____

_____

_____

_____

When we arrest our emotions, we will find rest.

_____

_____

_____

_____

_____

_____

_____

If you continue to stare at what you see, chances are you will not get what's to come.

_____

_____

_____

_____

_____

_____

_____

Love never ends. Memories of it only get better.

_____

_____

_____

_____

_____

_____

_____

Progress in a marriage can be compared to what brightness is to sunshine.

_____

_____

_____

_____

_____

_____

Soon is never early enough, but delay is better than zilch.

_____

_____

_____

_____

_____

_____

To avoid being misunderstood, we should listen slowly rather than thinking fast.

_____

_____

_____

_____

The fear of dying can hinder us from living.

We hear faith being discussed but hesitate to participate unless our name is called.

The presence of love will defeat the fear of rejection.

A fair exchange is not robbery.

It is a task to live what we believe, even harder to practice if there's doubt.

If you don't like what you've been thinking don't repeat it.

Liars may have full-time employment, but they have no benefits nor retirement.

Time has an agenda with a deadline. Only participants will benefit.

_____
_____
_____
_____
_____
_____
_____
_____

It is better to be early than too late. On time should be the norm.

_____
_____
_____
_____
_____
_____
_____

Do not take God for granted, he's watching. Check yourself before the tally.

_____

_____

_____

_____

_____

_____

People might not get from you what you gain from them, and that's determine by what's expected.

_____

_____

_____

_____

_____

_____

With all the people in the world, many are speechless due to loneliness.

_____

_____

_____

_____

_____

_____

Being alone is a condition, not a desire. If so, God would have not made Eve.

_____

_____

_____
_____
_____
_____
_____

God's greatest gift to mankind is love. Man's greatest gift to one another is sharing that love.

_____
_____
_____
_____
_____
_____
_____

The difference between tolerance and waiting is one you put up with and the other has a hopeful expectation.

Don't imprison yourself to your thoughts.

Avoid becoming your own bounty hunter.

The battery in your watch might stop, but not time.

It is a waste of time trying to impress God. Nobody can.

Often, we are so preoccupied and defensive with ourselves until we make allowances for not listening.

The quick fix for insecurity is confidence.

When we hearken unto the voice of the Lord, then we are able to speak to the mountain.

Three P's to balance your life: Peace, Patience and Power.

_____

_____

_____

_____

_____

_____

_____

Anything that keeps you up at night should be dealt with firmly and immediately the next day.

_____

_____

_____

_____

_____

_____

Even when we say I have nothing to say, we often go beyond what is necessary.

_____

_____

_____

_____

_____

_____

Authority may be questioned, but its influence is determined by the recipient.

_____

_____

Doubt is like a leaning tree with its roots above ground.

Being honest is an indicator that should not be ignored.

The first step to recovery is an extended hand and respect for mutual understanding.

Excuses are always appropriate for the user and are expected to be accepted from the listening party.

_____
_____
_____
_____
_____
_____
_____

Errors should never be used as a cover-up. Nor should they silence others.

_____
_____
_____
_____
_____
_____
_____

Get a room and a window before you confine your thoughts. There might not be another chance.

_____
_____
_____
_____
_____
_____
_____

God will always give you more than you ask for if you are willing to wait.

_____
_____
_____
_____
_____
_____
_____

Without compromise, there will never be a resolution.

_____
_____
_____
_____
_____
_____
_____

You can trust in God by giving him your worries.

_____
_____
_____
_____

When we don't have much time, we realize the importance of how to use it. When there seems to be ample time, we abuse it.

A welcome conversation is like background music; it gets your attention.

Endless talk becomes needless talk without willingness.

In the wedding vows it should read, God got everything under control, and we refuse to lose.

71

Reconciliation changes everything. Give and take can now find middle ground.

It would be a simple solution if we could put eye drops in the mouth so that we can see what others are saying.

When you refuse to compromise, you have only yourself to keep score.

Expressing your love is allowing your emotions to escape double jeopardy. Otherwise, the risk is never knowing the outcome.

_____

_____

_____

_____

_____

_____

A word of caution never ignores your inner voice.

_____

_____

_____

_____

_____

_____

There will be regrets in life but don't forget to apologize.

_____

_____

_____

_____

_____

_____

Requirements for friendship: an application, background check, interview, and a probational period.

_____

_____

_____

_____

If someone know what you don't know doesn't mean they know everything.

When nothing is said anything can be misinterpreted.

Don't delay, Father Time is never late.

About the Author

Reverend Dr. Linwood Best, with his wife Brenda, is pastor emeritus after more than thirty years of ministry. He is affectionately called Dr. B. because of his continued involvement and genuine concern for those in the community.

Academic bedrock: Northwest Florida State College, Shaw Divinity School, North Carolina Central University, Christian Bible College, and Dallas Theological Seminary.

It is his belief that we should never be too busy to listen attentively to those in need. He has a personal quote of "learn to listen and listen to learn." What a lesson to learn.

Words Are Powerful

"Gentle words bring life and health; a deceitful tongue crushes the spirit."
"Kind words are like honey – sweet to the soul and healthy for the body."
"Death and life are in the power of the tongue, and those who love it will eat its fruit." While words can injure, they can also build each other up."

"The Sovereign LORD has given me a well-instructed tongue, to know the word that sustains the weary. He wakens me morning by morning, wakens my ear to listen like one being instructed."

"A man hath joy by the answer of his mouth: and a word *spoken* in due season, how good *is it*!"

Words can provide much more than we give thought to. Words combined make up lyrics, verses, and choruses. Words are spoken in many languages. Words based on translation and culture can mean different things with, of course, different interpretations and opinions. Unfortunately, words can result in arguments, disagreements, disputes, and confrontations.

However, words can heal, mend, restore, and forgive but most importantly the word love can cover a multitude of sins. The communication of words can transform yesterday and give rise to new beginnings. Let's learn to listen and listen to learn.

Also, from Empower Publishing

by Linwood Best

Best "Quotes"

Best "Saying"

Best "Thoughts on Paper"